Robe

612-251-7766

robtsicora@gmail.com

LEADERSHIP
TRUST
BUILD IT, KEEP IT

IDEAS INTO ACTION SERIES

This series of books draws on the practical knowledge that the Center for Creative Leadership (CCL®) has generated, since its inception in 1970, through its research and educational activity conducted in partnership with hundreds of thousands of managers and executives. Much of this knowledge is shared—in a way that is distinct from the typical university department, professional association, or consultancy. CCL is not simply a collection of individual experts, although the individual credentials of its staff are impressive; rather it is a community, with its members holding certain principles in common and working together to understand and generate practical responses to today's leadership and organizational challenges.

The purpose of the series is to provide managers with specific advice on how to complete a developmental task or solve a leadership challenge. In doing that, the series carries out CCL's mission to advance the understanding, practice, and development of leadership for the benefit of society worldwide. We think you will find the Ideas Into Action Series an important addition to your leadership toolkit.

LEADERSHIP
TRUST
BUILD IT, KEEP IT

Christopher Evans

Center for
Creative
Leadership

IDEAS INTO ACTION SERIES

Aimed at managers and executives who are concerned with their own and others'
development, each book in this series gives specific advice on how to complete a
developmental task or solve a leadership problem.

LEAD CONTRIBUTOR
Christopher Evans

CONTRIBUTORS
Allan Calarco
Harold Scharlatt
Jonathan Vehar

DIRECTOR OF ASSESSMENTS, TOOLS, AND PUBLICATIONS
Sylvester Taylor

MANAGER, PUBLICATION DEVELOPMENT
Peter Scisco

EDITOR
Stephen Rush

ASSOCIATE EDITOR
Shaun Martin

DESIGN, LAYOUT, AND COVER DESIGN
Ed Morgan, navybluedesign.com

RIGHTS AND PERMISSIONS
Kelly Lombardino

EDITORIAL BOARD
**David Altman, Elaine Bleich, Regina Eckert, Joan Gurvis,
Jennifer Habig, Kevin Liu, Kelly Lombardino, Neal Maillet,
Jennifer Martineau, Portia Mount, Laura Santana, Harold Scharlatt**

CCL No. 00463

978-1-60491-602-7 – Print
978-1-60491-603-4 – Ebook

Center for Creative Leadership
www.ccl.org

The discussion of the Fist Five decision-making process on pages 24–25
is adapted with permission from "Making Implementable Decisions" by
Isabelle Rimanoczy and Tony Pearson, 2005. *LIM News*, 61, 2–6. ©2005
by Leadership in International Management

Illustrations: © yayayoyo www.fotosearch.com

CONTENTS

What Is Trust?

At its core, trust is an assurance that lets people manage risk in their relationships with others. As a decision mechanism, trust frees people to work closely together, and a lack of trust keeps reminding them to remain guarded. People seldom even think about the role trust plays when they interact with others—until some element of risk emerges in those relationships. When leaders take charge of how they deal with trust in everyday personal interactions, they gain control over a powerful tool for moving their initiatives forward, enhancing their collaborative efforts, and improving execution across their organizations.

Think about a time when you simply could not trust someone or were uncomfortable sharing responsibility for an important project with him or her. Write a few brief notes on the following questions:

What was the situation in which the lack of trust emerged?

_____

_____

What did this person do to fail to win your trust? What was your history with him or her?

_____

_____

What did this lack of trust feel like to you?

_____

_____

Jenna's Journey: Part One

From Jenna's perspective, every team meeting was the same. Eighty percent of the time was spent complaining or blaming, and the rest of the time was spent just inching along on the project until things reached crisis stage. Jenna didn't want to transfer to another division and disrupt her learning or her career, but something had to be done. As she made notes about her team experiences, some issues—both positive and negative—emerged:

Positives	Negatives
Stimulating projects	Lack of productivity during team meetings
Learning opportunities across the division	Poor or incomplete work results from some team members
New experiences to advance her career	Lack of support from the manager
	Conflicting work priorities among team members
	Need to work in crisis mode too often

Jenna shared these issues with the team in hopes that opening the negatives up for discussion would lead to an interest in solving them. She was wrong. The team members spent the rest of the discussion talking about whose challenges were greatest and how things never changed. When Jenna asked if they could take these issues seriously as a team she got reluctant approval from one person and a smile from another. But nothing changed.

To trust is to make yourself vulnerable to the actions of another, because you are in a relationship together. You might ask yourself during an encounter with someone in your organization whether you are willing to turn over your project, your deliverable, or some of your reputation to this person, knowing you could be disappointed or hurt by what he or she does.

To trust means making an active *choice* to risk something that's important to you or to your project that may have a lasting impact. In this way, trust and risk are two sides of the same coin.

People's experience of trust—how much they will trust—depends on the situation. You may be perfectly comfortable having a neighborhood high school student babysit your children when you go out to dinner, but you wouldn't trust her to make decisions about your retirement portfolio, nor would you want her to deliver the team presentation to your organization's senior leadership team. It's perfectly reasonable to trust someone in one situation but not in another. In fact, it's probably wise to do so.

> Leadership today is all about two words: It's all about truth and trust.
> —Jack Welch

3

Types of Trust

Trust is often thought of as having depth or degrees. And people often experience a range of trust—from a high level to a low level, or even an absence of trust. On the positive end of the scale, you may use words like *capable* or *highly confident.* The negative end of the scale calls to mind terms such as *distrust* (negative expectations regarding someone's conduct), *suspicion*, or even *betrayal.* Finally, some people view trust as necessarily including caution or safeguards.

This is called *bounded trust*—or, as President Reagan once famously remarked, "Trust, but verify."

When people think about trust in organizational life, the first place to ground themselves is in whom or what they are trusting. In most cases this is *interpersonal* trust—for example a one-to-one human relationship, as in one person trusting another person who might satisfy or disappoint the trusting individual with his or her actions. In the workplace this "person" is often a group or department—for example, senior leadership, which must be trusted to take care of its employees. Even though senior leadership is actually a group, when they act as people making decisions about people it is considered an interpersonal relationship.

The most common framework for interpersonal trust uses expectancy theory—the idea that trust is based on beliefs and expectations about someone's intentions or performance and on the trusting individual's emotional security surrounding those beliefs. In other words, it's like a transaction between two people. And the higher the stakes for the trusting individual, the more building of trust may be required. In some cases and with some people, trust needs to be given in order to earn it in return.

Sometimes people deal with *system trust*, or trust (or lack thereof) that an impersonal structure, such as a federal government or a monetary system, is sound. For instance, they might have a high level of trust that the Postal Service will deliver their mail, but they might have a lower level of trust that the Social Security system will still be viable when they try to collect on their years of deposits upon retirement.

Most of the trust issues faced by leaders involve interpersonal trust, and these show up in all facets of their relationships. Stephen M. R. Covey, an organizational consultant and author of *The Speed of Trust: The One Thing That Changes Everything*, describes what happens when trust issues are not resolved: Low trust is costly to an organization because it impacts speed and cost, taxes relationships, saps productivity and creativity, and makes it impossible to sustain great results. Covey cites a 2002 study by global consulting firm Watson Wyatt Worldwide (which merged in 2010 with Towers Perrin to form Towers Watson) that showed that the total return to shareholders in high-trust organizations is almost three times higher than the return in low-trust organizations.

So if trust issues are so prevalent and important, logic and emotion suggest that leaders should approach them as strategically as possible.

Dimensions of Trust

When leaders say that they need to build *trust* among their middle managers, the term trust often means different things to different individuals or groups. Sometimes there are differing perceptions, perceived causes, or desired outcomes, yet most leaders tend to work simply with that one word—*trust*. But having a common language and understanding among the parties involved helps them identify what they mean when some aspect of a relationship, behavior, or performance is amiss.

In the article "An Integrative Model of Organizational Trust" by Roger C. Mayer, James H. Davis, and F. David Schoorman, the authors describe trust as embodying distinct elements of ability, benevolence, and integrity. What they call *factors of perceived trustworthiness*—dimensions of trust—can appear as three different kinds of trust; more precisely there are three distinct elements of human reasoning that each relate to one's willingness to be vulnerable in a given situation. This helps people focus on which aspects of individual or team behavior or performance are working well and which are not. In adapting the work of the article's authors for a global audience, this book uses the term *loyalty* rather than *benevolence*, because *loyalty* captures the essence of the relationship and will be more readily understood by more readers.

Figure 1

Dimensions of Trust

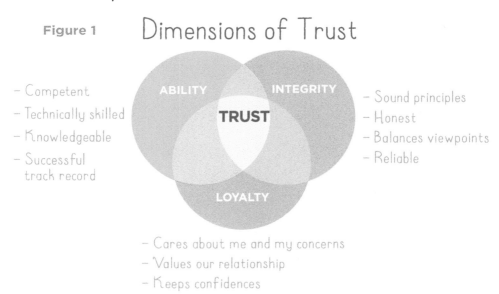

- Competent
- Technically skilled
- Knowledgeable
- Successful track record

ABILITY   INTEGRITY

TRUST

LOYALTY

- Sound principles
- Honest
- Balances viewpoints
- Reliable

- Cares about me and my concerns
- Values our relationship
- Keeps confidences

Ability is about technical skills, competencies, and execution. Whenever people ask if someone is able, capable, or skilled, or if he or she can accomplish a specific task, they are considering ability. People interact with one another as leaders, supervisors, and coworkers, and they see technical, interpersonal, and leadership competencies enacted at various skill levels at different levels in the organization. And everyone has seen that people may have expertise in some areas but not in others.

When leaders make judgments about ability—remembering that trust is always specific to the situation—they often think of the skills that lead to effective outcomes for the particular assignment or project. In other words: "Can he do it?" "Does she know the right steps?"

Here's an example: Walter has offered to write the design architecture for a new project plan, but his last three project designs have required significant rework by the team. Do you as Walter's manager trust his ability to write a design architecture that won't need significant rework?

Following are some examples of questions that can help you gauge aspects of ability that might influence the degree of trust you experience during an interaction.

- Can she do what I'm asking her to do?
- Does the team possess the knowledge and understanding of the processes to produce this work?
- What might he need to learn in order to accomplish this task?
- What help might he need to get this done?
- How well did she perform the most recent similar task?

Integrity includes shared values (for example, principles, fairness, and character) and expectations (for example, reliability and consistency) between the parties. When people think about a wise and principled leader, someone esteemed for living the principles they admire, for their tenacity, and for their consistent successes, they are thinking about integrity. They often see humility and a rock-solid ethic to uphold what is true, right, and honorable, even when it makes the leader look a fool, which, oddly, isn't very often. They see someone they agree with in important ways.

When people make judgments about integrity they often think of *strong character*, *stability*, and *reliability*. Do I agree with the wisdom of his decisions? Can I count on her to deliver on her promise?

The following questions can help leaders gain clarity around aspects of integrity that might be affecting their perception of trust.

- Does her past behavior/history/reputation suggest unswerving, rather than self-serving, ethics?

- Does he deal evenly with others on his projects or does he sometimes have favorites?

- Do I agree with the soundness of his approach on this challenge, and is he open to discussing it?

- What about her as a leader do I really admire? What values do we share?

- Do we agree about what we're discussing?

- Will he do what he says? Can I count on him, even as busy as he is?

Loyalty is related to truth-telling and a personal relationship between the trustor and trustee. People are considering the trust dimension of loyalty whenever they think about personal connections with others and whether those others will support them or abandon them in tough situations. They wonder if others will maintain a confidence, keep a secret, or protect them rather than take advantage of and point the blame at them, or if they will support their well-being and development. In the more extreme cases of perceived trust abandonment, betrayal shows up.

When leaders make judgments about loyalty they are thinking of such a relationship. Will she keep this matter private? Can I count on him to support me on this?

The following questions can help leaders gain clarity around aspects of loyalty that might be affecting their perception of trust.

- Can I confide in her on this?
- If things go wrong for both of us on this decision, will he accept responsibility with me?
- To what extent does he care about me and my ideas?
- Will he restructure my work so I can get experience in this new area?
- Does she see her promise to me as a priority among her other work commitments?
- Is he willing to put his commitment to me on this matter ahead of his personal goals?
- Do we have a relationship to be able to discuss this when conflicts arise rather than to let commitments slip?

With a common way to talk about the specific behaviors that lead to trust concerns in the workplace, leaders can engage in productive, solution-based discussions. All parties can now work toward the same understanding of what can create trust challenges in work interactions. But you may not be ready to meet with your colleague just yet.

Trust issues may not arise solely in one dimension; sometimes what's not working well may be a combination of factors. Curiosity is a valuable mind-set that can help you see things more clearly, more closely to what the situation really is. Spending some time to become clear about your own understanding of the underlying trust concerns is often worthwhile and can make the difference in mounting an effective response to your concerns. Meeting with a thought partner or trusted adviser may also add insight to challenge your assumptions and initial conclusions.

> **Trust is the lubrication that makes it possible for organizations to work.**
> — Warren Bennis

Jenna's Journey: Part Two

Jenna was becoming depressed about continuing more of these counterproductive team meetings in the future. She decided to try to make productive change where she could, within her sphere of influence. She asked herself: What's at the root of my dissatisfaction with the team? After drawing up pages of notes she wrote down the following: I have no energy to work on this team; I don't look forward to this work.

While these issues were preying on her she overheard the end of a hallway conversation between a peer leader in another division, Paul, and one of his teammates, Julian.

Paul said: "Julian, this presentation is going to be used by senior leadership and I need to be able to trust you on this. You won't let me down, will you?"

"No, I won't," was the response.

"Thanks very much, and I look forward to getting your report."

For Jenna, a connection was made. She did research on the concept of trust in organizational life and then spent some time diagramming her team's challenges using the trust framework.

Jenna's Team Challenge	Trust Dimensions
Lack of productivity during team meetings	Team processes (ability, integrity)
Poor or incomplete work product from some team members	Skill (ability), priorities (loyalty)
Lack of support from our manager	Loyalty
Conflicting work priorities with team members	Priorities (loyalty)
Need to work in crisis mode too often	Team processes (ability, integrity)

Jenna shared some content on trust issues in organizations and her map of the team's challenges. She asked for permission to openly discuss the team's performance issues in hopes of improving not only team performance but also the team members' satisfaction with working together. This time most of the team agreed.

Taking Action on Trust Issues

Think back to the notes you wrote down on page 1 about the situation where you could not trust someone. What dimension of trust was the most prominent in that situation? Was it related to ability, integrity, or loyalty—or a combination of them? How does your view of the underlying trust issue open up a new understanding of, or options for, dealing with the real cause of your lack of trust?

Having a common language to be able to talk about trust is the starting point for taking clear actions when your level of trust is low. To make this useful, people have to be able to get trust conversations out in the open, to make them more visible and safe.

It's also critical to be able to talk about which behaviors and approaches are not helping the collective work, while supporting and upholding the valuable contributions from the team or employees. There needs to be a common language around the trust issues stemming from ability, integrity, and loyalty.

But before we look at trust conversations between individuals and teams, we must examine a related tool: *feedback.*

You need to be skilled at using a number of tools in your leadership toolkit and to know when to use each tool. And while a trust issue may have its root in performance or behavior, don't substitute a periodic feedback discussion when the situation suggests the need for a deeper conversation on trust. Let's take a look at the differences.

For our purposes, feedback is defined as information received in response to actions taken or behaviors shown to others. The key to effective feedback is creating and delivering a specific message based on observed behavior. The feedback you give should enable the receiver to walk away understanding exactly what he or she did and what effect it had on you. When the result is this specific and this direct, there is a better chance that the person receiving the feedback will be motivated to begin, continue, or stop behaviors that affect performance. Giving feedback should be part of your daily communications to encourage both the continuance of effective behavior and an understanding of the impact of ineffective approaches and actions.

So if the performance of direct reports or peers is less than expected, effective feedback will help them understand why you feel as you do and will give them the opportunity to do better next time.

The need for a trust conversation with someone tends to build up over time. It's often the result of not having a practiced culture in the organization of giving feedback or because giving feedback is not a regular practice of the individual leader. When leaders avoid giving feedback to coworkers or teams over time, the problems are not normally self-correcting; they build up.

Trust issues flow from a behavior or performance problem. When people feel uncomfortable about sharing responsibility or have low expectations of the timeliness or quality of a delivered product, they're dealing with a trust issue. To solve that pervasive problem requires going beyond performance feedback and entering into a trust conversation.

Part of this is because the lack of trust ends up being the conclusion drawn as a result of concerns about ability, integrity, and loyalty. A conversation is needed in which the broad concerns and ramifications of the lack of trust are clearly stated and the specific behaviors or root causes are shared. As with feedback, this sharing needs to be focused enough to be unimpeachable: The effect of low trust is a feeling or conclusion held by the trustor that the trustee cannot deny.

So with direct reports, it's time for a trust conversation when your honest attempts at feedback haven't changed unacceptable behavior. Derailment is possible—with career development about to stall or a job in jeopardy. With peers, a trust conversation may be needed when your feedback hasn't changed behavior or you just feel a relationship isn't working.

So feedback is both a stand-alone leadership tool and the means for entering a trust conversation. With this conversation starter, you can begin to uncover the real causes of your trust concerns.

"It's Hard to Put My Trust in Others"

Let's listen in on a conversation between a project leader, Ethan, and his coach, Karl.

Ethan: "Years ago I let some team members do their part on a project that ended up a disaster, and I almost got fired. Ever since then I've had a need to control my projects to make sure they're done well. It's *my* reputation on the line and it's hard to put my trust in others who won't do the same job I can do."

Karl: "Are you telling me you have all the time necessary to get all your work done?"

Ethan: "No, of course not; I have to oversee so many projects closely, like the Chartman project we discussed during our last call."

Karl: "Ethan, I hear two things from you. First is that you can't possibly get done all the things you need to do. Second, I hear your need to oversee or manage many projects closely, which is time-consuming and takes you away from your other work. Seeing that you cannot do both of these things well, what would you need to have in place on the Chartman project to be more comfortable letting go some of that constant oversight?"

Ethan: "I would like my team to deliver an impressive product design and I would like Grahame to ensure his people gave us a fully scoped and researched project plan, but I can't rely on either of them at this point."

Karl: "So when you say you can't rely on them, this sounds like a trust issue to me. You can't trust that they'll produce a product design that you'll be comfortable with. What steps could you take to make that happen?"

Ethan: "For my team, I think biweekly project reviews would keep me informed and let me guide them along. For Grahame's team, I would have to have his assurance that we both understand the project needs, deliverables, and time frames. I could meet with him about this, and I could have my team leads set up a project-review system with his team."

Karl: "If you did these things, how will you and your people benefit from this approach compared with what you do now?"

Ethan: "I suppose I would be helping my people be more accountable and independent. It might improve my relationship with Grahame, by reaching out to him rather than blaming his team for not being able to read my mind. For myself, I suppose it would help me remember that I have a choice in how I address these issues. Now I have to go do it."

Karl: "And if you run into barriers?"

Ethan: "I would sit down and work out what I need to feel comfortable with letting go of some control and still get the outcome I require."

Individual Trust Conversations

Getting trust out in the open makes it safe to raise these concerns between people and in the team. In approaching a trust conversation with an individual, consider an opening such as:

- "I'd like to talk about something that's concerning me."
- "May we talk about your work on the project?"
- "I need to explore with you where we are on the project."

Let's look in on Maria opening up a trust conversation with her new hire, Alain.

"Alain, I really have to talk to you about your reliability. There isn't any concern about your ability—you can do this work, and I sense that you want to do well here. However, you promised to get the work to me on Monday morning and it's now Thursday afternoon and it's not done. I just need you to deliver on your promises. It's disappointing me, holding the team back, and I'm beginning to sense a reluctance among your peers to work with you."

In the CCL-developed Situation–Behavior–Impact model for giving effective feedback, behavior-changing potential arises when the employee understands the impact his or her behavior is having on someone else or on the team. In the trust conversation starter above, Maria is clear about which of Alain's behaviors (reliability/integrity) threaten to derail his career. She upholds his ability by saying he can do the work and his loyalty by saying she feels he wants to do well in his new role. She's building her own trustability by showing genuine support (loyalty) for Alain and by executing her own leadership responsibilities and adhering to her values (integrity).

One natural response to criticism is defensiveness. Maria doesn't shy away from her tough message but neither does she diminish it through her support of Alain. She doesn't use the sandwich method of providing feedback by sharing something positive, something negative, and something positive again, potentially leaving Alain confused about her intention. Notice also that Maria doesn't say she does not trust Alain, even though trust is the issue. In the first stage of discussion she enters gently enough to remain in partnership with him. By keeping Alain's lack of reliability as the main message she stays focused on what she must accomplish in the conversation. She also sets up the beginning of a productive, outcomes-oriented leadership coaching conversation.

His Heart Is In the Right Place. His Ability Is Not.

Henri is truly a nice man: pleasant, helpful, and unassuming. The kind of person you'd want on your work team except for one thing: He hasn't done independent work as a team member. His reports have been quickly written but insufficiently researched, his arguments poorly supported, and his conclusions often superficial. His manager, Aru, has given him specific feedback on the impact of his performance on several occasions. Aru now finds himself beginning to review Henri's progress at multiple stages in order to ensure he is producing usable work product for the team. Aru has decided Henri is close to derailing and it is time to have a trust talk to get the issue out in the open.

Aru: "Henri, you and I are spending a lot of time in periodic review of your projects. We've spoken now several times about the kind of work outcomes you've been producing versus what we need from someone in your role. I need you to be functioning more independently in terms of your processes and the quality of your work products. Can you tell me how you think you're going to accomplish this?"

Henri: "Aru, I'm breaking my back on these projects, doing everything you tell me to do. What else should I be doing?"

Aru: "Let me be clear, it's not your heart or your dedication. I truly respect your attitude and wish more people were as dedicated as you; it's the work product. As you and I have discussed before, you only touch the surface of the issues and miss important elements and connections when you do your background work. In most cases the data is there in our system, but you're not accessing it or relating it to the challenge and potential solutions. We've talked about this in the last two projects."

Henri: "Not all of this is a surprise to me, but I thought I was doing well enough. What are you saying to me?"

Aru: "I'm saying that if I could trust you to produce high-quality, researched work you would be positioned for rapid promotion. But that's not the case now. I want you on my team, but you and I have to get clear about what acceptable work product looks like and you need to apply yourself to it."

Henri: "What would you say to teaming me with Paco on the upcoming Chartman account so I can see his approach to the work. Then I can sit down with you periodically and share my observations and what connections I'm making between your feedback today and what you want from me in the future. Does that sound reasonable to you?"

Aru: "That sounds great. Look, I'm on your side, but this is beyond giving you some routine performance feedback. This is a trust issue, and I want to trust you—and you're the one who's going to have to be able to do the work. Now I'd like you to send me a short e-mail outlining what we just talked about and we'll both be clear and have no surprises the next time we meet."

Team Trust Conversations

When a leader harbors negative expectations (distrust) that the team's progress is likely to remain lackluster because of people or process problems, it's time for a trust conversation. Opening up a trust conversation in a work team is more complex than with an individual because you're sharing your concern among multiple people. You're suggesting an opportunity for improvement, or even that an outright performance problem exists. That opinion might not be shared by others, particularly anyone who enjoys controlling the team's work, so proceed carefully. Checking your assumptions, conclusions, and approach with a fellow team member or thought partner may help avoid missteps and ultimately assist you in building community around your team's collaborative work.

As with individual trust concerns, it's important that you be clear about the nature of the trust issue. What's not working as well as it should? Could the cause of the problem be at the team level, a problem with how teamwork is conducted, or is it really a trust issue around one or more individual members? Taking time to think through your concerns about how the team functions related to trust is important. You want your leadership interactions with the team to be fruitful and to improve your team's performance, so you don't want to begin with an erroneous premise and diminish your chances for improvement.

To determine whether the root issue is at the team or individual level, consider Figure 2.

Figure 2

Team or Individual Trust Issue?

Team Behaviors	Individual Behaviors
Poor/incomplete work from several members	Poor/incomplete work from a single member
Conflicting work priorities outside the team	Conflicting work priorities outside the team
Need to work in crisis mode too often	Work, when done, is submitted at the last moment
No team norms around performance expectations	Excuses provided or "always busy"
Team roles are not clearly defined or understood	Seeks own agenda or approach regularly
Members don't listen well to others	Individual doesn't listen well to others
Team tasks not clearly defined	Says individual assignment wasn't clear
Lack of support from manager/team sponsor	
No frequent feedback to members regarding performance	

One indicator that your concern is a team trust issue is how the team conducts its meetings and monitors its operations. If the team's meetings are unfocused and there never seems to be much progress made from meeting to meeting, you might point out that the team seems to have no common agreement on performance expectations. You'll want to approach the topic clearly and cogently.

In approaching the topic of trust within a team, consider an opening such as:

- "I feel like we're missing something important in how we're doing our team work."
- "I think we're each approaching the team's work with different priorities."
- "There are some aspects of the team's work that are working well and others that aren't."
- "I feel like we need to gain some clarity around team issues that are keeping the team from executing better."

Trust and Decision-Making

When working with teams, leaders have the opportunity to observe how teams make decisions. In most cases they will discover that there is no explicit process for making decisions. Most of the time an implicit and unclear majority rule is used. What does this mean? A person suggests something and looks around to see if there is general agreement or disagreement. Agreement is not explicitly sought. If there are no objections, it is interpreted as agreement.

Experience shows that people do not voice objections for a variety of different reasons:

- They are still thinking.
- They haven't fully understood the proposal or don't think a decision is being made.
- They want to see if others have objections before they state theirs.
- There is a certain intimidation factor because of the person who made the suggestion (it could be a strong leader, an authority figure, a friend, a strong advocate, or someone they don't want to get into conflict with).
- They have doubts but don't feel comfortable raising them.
- They lack clarity on whether they are supposed to voice concerns or are allowed to.
- They're waiting to be asked for their opinion.

All these reasons may lie behind the silence—a silence with potentially dangerous impact on the implementation of decisions reached. The danger lies in the fact that those who fail to express their views at the time of the decision will express them later during the implementation of the decision. This might end up postponing implementation, blocking it, or reducing the motivation of the silent ones to execute the decision, which then destroys trust.

The Fist Five is a decision-making process based on consensus, in which everyone is able to express his or her thoughts about a decision in a simultaneous voting process. Fist Five is not based on complete agreement. Consensus is defined here as a process of discussion in which group members talk, sense, and think together, resulting in a decision that everyone can ultimately support. Consensus is recommended as the best means of making decisions for most teams and, importantly, it lays the groundwork for trust.

The Fist Five provides positive ownership for decisions, it encourages a healthy dialogue, and it allows issues to surface and be aired. Because it is announced, people become aware that a decision is about to be made; this forces those involved in the decision to express clearly what the proposal is. As people are asked to express what is behind their votes, new information is brought into the room to be considered and discussed.

Finally, no decision is made until the objections are resolved and the issue is ready for implementation.

Here's how the Fist Five works: The person who has a proposal to be decided on spells it out in a way that clearly establishes the essence of the proposal. For example, "I propose that we hire a new PR advisor."

The person making the proposal gives the team members half a minute to reflect, then asks them to raise their hands and use their fingers to vote on the degree to which they agree with the proposal, according to the scale shown in Figure 3:

Figure 3

The Fist Five

FIST
I can't live with the decision; I will block it or leave the group.

ONE
I don't like it but I won't block it.
Don't count on me for a lot of energy.

TWO
I'm not excited by the decision, but I will do some work to support it.

THREE
I think the decision is okay; I will get involved.

FOUR
I think the decision is good; I will work hard to support it.

FIVE
I think the decision is great; I may leave the group if it is not made.

25

By using this method to visually test the potential for consensus, everyone can see where everyone else is on the decision continuum.

The next step is for the person who made the proposal to ask the voters on opposite ends of the spectrum (those who gave it a fist or a one and those who gave it a four or a five) to express what is behind their thinking. This will uncover and bring in new information that should be included in the process.

Sometimes people are opposed to a decision but do not know exactly why. They can't give a good rationale and say, "I just don't think this is the right decision." A way to help such people explore their thoughts (which may not even be conscious to them) is to ask, "What has to be true for you to accept this decision?" or, "What would you need in order to change your vote from a two to a three?" This allows these individuals to contribute information that illuminates their thinking.

This process may be more time-consuming than a simple majority vote but it enriches the decision and ultimately makes its implementation easier. The team will come to a new consensus or make a different and better decision.

Jenna's Journey: Part Three

When Jenna began her discussion saying she had no energy and was getting burned out working on the team's challenges, it was like a burden had been lifted from the team. Sensing this, she said she thought that a lack of trust might be one root of the team's performance issues. What ensued was an objective discussion about what was working well and what wasn't in each of the three trust dimensions—ability, integrity, and loyalty—without blaming anyone for their individual performance. She let the content of the discussion guide each member to see his or her own parts in the team's performance. The team agreed that a lively outburst of "Trust issue!" could be grounds for pausing team conversations and exploring any concerns they faced.

   This approach also led the team to reach out to its manager about the lack of support the team felt at times. Impressed with the work the team had done on using trust as a guiding framework, he agreed to be subject to the "Trust issue!" cry when he was needed to support the team.

Last Words

Following are some focused questions and statements you can use to initiate trust conversations with your team:

- What consensus do we have in terms of the skills needed to address this issue? (Ability)

- I'd like each of us to confirm which aspects of our project responsibilities we might need help with to stay on schedule. (Ability)

- Is anyone unclear about his or her tasks or responsibilities before our next meeting? (Ability)

- Looking at our team processes, does each of us feel we're contributing to the team's work? (Integrity)

- On a scale of 0 to 5, how open are we being with each other as a team? (Integrity)

- On a scale of 0 to 5, how well does each of us believe we are performing individually in meeting our commitments on this project? (Integrity)

- We're missing our internal deadlines, so I'd like everyone to confirm his or her work priorities outside the team to help us get back on target. (Loyalty)

- I've sensed a drop in enthusiasm on this project. I'd like to check in with everyone to see where this work falls on his or her priorities. (Loyalty)

Here are some other questions you can ask to help build your leadership communication skills and your managerial courage regarding discussions of trust:

- What is the issue (context)?
- Who is involved (person or team)?
- What dimension(s) of trust are involved?
- What's my approach?
- Who can be my thought partner on this?

Focused trust conversations achieve a number of things:

- They go beyond feedback conversations in helping leaders create the setting for lasting performance, by addressing behaviors and performance challenges that detract from building value.
- They target what's not working well and allow the parties to discover workable solutions.
- They are developmental; they uphold and affirm what is working well.

Leaders who initiate trust conversations help coworkers and teams learn to discuss deep performance issues. This helps enhance individual, team, and organizational effectiveness. Spending time learning how to gain clarity around root problems related to trust gives leaders practice in developing their influencing skills and can make the difference between success and failure.

Glossary

Bounded Trust—A perception of the limits the trustor places on the trustee.

Consensus—The result of a process of discussion in which members talk, sense, and think together, leading to a decision that everyone can ultimately support.

Dimensions of Trust

- **Ability**—The group of skills, competencies, and characteristics that enable a party to have influence within a specific domain.
- **Integrity**—A trustor's perception that the trustee adheres to a set of principles that the trustor finds acceptable.
- **Loyalty**—The extent to which a trustee is believed to want to do good for the trustor.

Distrust—Negative expectations regarding the conduct of another.

Feedback—Information received in response to actions or behaviors.

High Level of Trust—Strong confidence in the ability, integrity, and loyalty of a trustee.

Interpersonal Trust—Trust between individuals or, in some cases, between groups of people in which actions are seen as people relating to people.

Low Level of Trust—Limited confidence in the ability, integrity, and loyalty of a trustee.

System Trust—A form of trust in which the trustee is an impersonal system, such as a government, organized function, or business.

Trust—A willingness to be vulnerable to the actions of another party.

Trusting Behaviors—Those actions of ability, integrity, and loyalty that a trustor values and that a trustee performs in a given trust situation.

Vulnerability—A feeling of powerlessness in regard to the actions that others take that affect you or your interests.

Willingness to Trust—A trustor's evaluation of the trustee's ability, integrity, and loyalty as a result of logical and emotional discernment in a specific trust situation.

Suggested Resources

Butler, J. K. (1991). Toward understanding and measuring conditions of trust: Evolution of a conditions of trust inventory. *Journal of Management, 17*, 643–663.

Covey, S. M. R. (2005). *The speed of trust: The one thing that changes everything.* New York, NY: The Free Press.

Cummings, L., & Bromiley, P. (1996). The Organizational Trust Inventory (OTI): Development and validation. In *Trust in organizations: Frontiers of theory and research.* (pp. 302–331). Thousand Oaks, CA: SAGE Publications.

Kanaga, K., & Browning, H. (2003). *Maintaining team performance.* Greensboro, NC: CCL Press.

Mayer, R. M., Davis, J. H., & Schoorman, F. D. (1995). An integrative model of organizational trust. *Academy of Management Review, 20*(3), 709–734.

Mishra, A. K., & Mishra, K. E. (2013). *Becoming a trustworthy leader: Psychology and practice.* New York, NY: Routledge.

Reina, D. S., & Reina, M. L. (1999). *Trust and betrayal in the workplace: Building effective relationships in your organization.* Oakland, CA: Berrett-Koehler.

Reina, D. S., & Reina, M. L. (2010). *Rebuilding trust in the workplace: Seven steps to renew confidence, commitment, and energy.* Oakland, CA: Berrett-Koehler.

Rimanoczy, I., & Pearson, T. (2005). Making implementable decisions. *LIM News, 61*, 2–6.

Weitzel, S. (2000). *Feedback that works: How to build and deliver your message.* Greensboro, NC: CCL Press.

NOTES

NOTES

NOTES

ABOUT THE CENTER FOR CREATIVE LEADERSHIP

The Center for Creative Leadership (CCL) is a top-ranked, global provider of leadership development. By leveraging the power of leadership to drive results that matter most to clients, CCL transforms individual leaders, teams, organizations, and society. Our array of cutting-edge solutions is steeped in extensive research and experience gained from working with hundreds of thousands of leaders at all levels. Ranked among the world's Top 5 providers of executive education by *Financial Times* and in the Top 10 by *Bloomberg BusinessWeek*, CCL has offices in Greensboro, NC; Colorado Springs, CO; San Diego, CA; Brussels, Belgium; Moscow, Russia; Addis Ababa, Ethiopia; Johannesburg, South Africa; Singapore; Gurgaon, India; and Shanghai, China.

Center for Creative Leadership

ORDERING INFORMATION